Rafael Rangel Szillat

Augmented Reality - Interactive tool for learning LIBRAS

Rafael Rangel Szillat

Augmented Reality - Interactive tool for learning LIBRAS

ScienciaScripts

Imprint

Any brand names and product names mentioned in this book are subject to trademark, brand or patent protection and are trademarks or registered trademarks of their respective holders. The use of brand names, product names, common names, trade names, product descriptions etc. even without a particular marking in this work is in no way to be construed to mean that such names may be regarded as unrestricted in respect of trademark and brand protection legislation and could thus be used by anyone.

Cover image: www.ingimage.com

This book is a translation from the original published under ISBN 978-3-330-19778-7.

Publisher:
Sciencia Scripts
is a trademark of
Dodo Books Indian Ocean Ltd. and OmniScriptum S.R.L publishing group

120 High Road, East Finchley, London, N2 9ED, United Kingdom
Str. Armeneasca 28/1, office 1, Chisinau MD-2012, Republic of Moldova, Europe
Printed at: see last page
ISBN: 978-620-8-23919-0

Development of an augmented reality animation portal for the teaching-learning process of the Brazilian Sign Language - LIBRAS.

Rafael Rangel Szillat
Federal Institute of Education, Science and Technology of Bahia, Salvador, Brazil

Summary

People with hearing loss (HL), due to a lack of accessibility, encounter difficulties in the teaching-learning process and social inclusion. As a result, technologies are being developed to help this section of society, in order to make their lives easier and more enjoyable. Among many technologies, Augmented Reality (AR) has been used as an aid to the teaching-learning process, by increasing interaction between deaf students and with the Brazilian Sign Language (LIBRAS) teaching method. This project aims to create a free educational portal to encourage the study of LIBRAS through AR and thus innovate the teaching method for students with hearing loss. The aim of this article is to demonstrate a portal that uses AR to teach LIBRAS.

Keywords: LIBRAS; Augmented Reality; Teaching and learning; Deafness.

1. Introduction

According to the World Health Organization (2017), more than 5% of the world's population, which amounts to more than 360 million people, has some form of hearing loss. This corresponds to around 328 million adults and 32 million children. People who suffer from this disorder, especially when it is inherited in childhood or at birth, need special attention to learn how to communicate.

This care needs to come from families and teachers, who need to adapt in order to be able to deal with people suffering from deafness from an early age. This concern opens the door to better access to education, allowing deaf children to be more easily included in society.

Hearing loss (HL) hampers the overall development of children, especially their language (BARROS; GALINDO; JACOB, 2002). Difficulty communicating impairs the interaction of children with hearing loss and favors social isolation. In addition, the lack of accessibility, as well as the lack of didactic and methodological adaptations, makes it difficult for these children to learn.

Limited access to basic services and social exclusion can have a significant impact on daily life, causing feelings of loneliness, isolation and frustration, particularly among older people with hearing loss (World Health Organization, 2017). One solution for integrating deaf or hard of hearing children into society is the use of Sign Language (SL).

Hearing is essential for the acquisition of oral language. The lack of this language influences both the mother's relationship with her child and creates gaps in the psychological processes of integrating experiences, causing emotional problems and the person's cognitive development. According to Redondo and Carvalho (2000) AD makes it difficult for the individual to interact with society and learn at school, especially if the institution is not prepared to deal with the student's linguistic uniqueness. According to Peixoto (2006):

"Sign language, historically so rejected, is now seen as a positive part of deaf people's lives, as an indispensable element in ensuring their appropriation of cultural elements, integration into society and access to knowledge - academic or otherwise - as well as good cognitive and affective development."

In Brazil, the sign language used by the deaf community is LIBRAS. According to FENEIS magazine (issue 2:16), LIBRAS, like all sign languages, is a gestural-visual modality because it uses gestural movements (SINAL)[1] and facial expressions, which are perceived by sight, as a channel or means of communication.

Just like spoken language, sign languages are not universal. Each country has its own sign language(s). These have all the linguistic aspects of a natural language, such as the linguistic variation that occurs through historical and regional influences on speech. In view of this fact, the project in question sought to teach LIBRAS, taking into account the signs used in Bahia, more specifically in the city of Salvador.

People with hearing loss define themselves as deaf because they interact and understand the world through visual experiences, expressing their culture mainly through the use of LIBRAS. Deaf people find it difficult to enter the social sphere and develop well academically, because the people around them don't always know this type of language. Thus, learning LIBRAS is a way of integrating this population into communication, reducing the restrictions caused by the language barrier.

Bearing in mind the lack of teaching and learning methods for LIBRAS, not only for deaf people, but also for those who need to know the language in order to communicate with them, innovative structures that encourage learning are being sought in the educational sphere. In this way, technology can be used in favor of

---

It's important to note that the gestural movements to which FENEIS Magazine refers are not the hand gestures that we all make when we speak orally and move our hands in order to express mimicry and pantomime, but are an integral part of our communication system. In this case, "gestural movements" refer to the SIGN, i.e. the word of visuospatial languages. According to Bento (2010, p. 30), "the signs of visuospatial languages, [...] belong to the set of minimal units that form larger units and are formed from the combination of the phonological parameters of hand configuration, location, movement, hand orientation and non-manual expressions, in this way, they are conventional, that is, they have meanings combined by a social group".

education.

Recent research suggests that even with qualified interpreters in the integrated classroom, educators need to understand that deaf children learn differently. They learn more easily from visual information and often process information differently than hearing boys and girls.

For centuries, deaf children have not been educated in the same way as their hearing peers, which is why they suffer more learning difficulties. Even today, there are no schools to teach deaf children in many countries (Livadas, 2013).

Thousands of deaf and hard-of-hearing students, from toddlers to college students, were evaluated in Australia, the Netherlands, England, Scotland and on the campus of Rochester Institute of Technology (RIT) in New York, to determine how they acquire new knowledge and how that knowledge is organized, understood and communicated to others. This study evaluated everything from eye-movement tracking and memory tasks performed by the student to participation in experimental "lessons" taught by deaf and hearing teachers. From this evaluation, it was visibly evident that deaf children assimilated visual and three-dimensional forms better, while normal children picked up more information from their environment and from the words and noises they heard (Livadas, 2013).

Other studies on the deaf state that deaf students who perform better academically are generally those whose parents communicated effectively with them from an early age. Early language skills - sign language and spoken language - correlate with reading ability, with no evidence that one is necessarily better than the other.

The majority of deaf students with reading difficulties have difficulty understanding SL, which stems from their parents' lack of language education from an early age. As a result, when they enter school, they are often behind other children in their knowledge of the world, number concepts and problem-solving skills, and not just in language. Deaf students don't always learn or think in the same way as non-deaf children, so they need differentiated attention (Livadas, 2013).

Now that we've described some of the differences in how deaf and hard-of-hearing students learn, it's important to know how to turn this knowledge into more effective teaching strategies.

Another study, carried out in Sweden, of deaf or hard-of-hearing children raised in a bi-bi (bilingual and/or bicultural) environment, who were exposed to Swedish sign language from an early age, as well as writing and/or speaking Swedish from a young age, showed that they had the same language development as a (hearing) Swede who was bilingual in two languages. Other studies of deaf teenagers who were raised in bi-lingual classrooms showed that they graduated from high school with reading and math scores comparable to their peers without LD (Mitchell, 2011).

Therefore, communication is an important tool in early childhood education. Deaf people can have the same opportunity to learn and are just as intelligent as hearing people. Based on this statement, it is necessary to create innovative methods, integrating deaf children in communication and socialization. This article presents a new methodology for teaching SL. In order to inspire users of this language to learn in a fun way, using an interactive and dynamic method.

It's important to emphasize that LS is different all over the world. Just as there is variation in spoken English and Portuguese, or in the accent between different regions, LS varies from language to language and from region to region. This work was structured and evaluated by LIBRAS teachers and students, focusing on the expressions of Salvador-BA.

In recent years, new ways have been created and/or improved to make it easier for people to access knowledge. Thanks to technology, more and more people can access information at any time they want, in a simple and easy way.

With the inclusion of children with hearing loss in mainstream schools, technology is a way of helping teachers in the teaching-learning process. As technology is already part of most Brazilian schools and homes, televisions and computers, among others, are already used as a means of communication and information. However, for Moran (1995), the presence of this technological apparatus in the classroom does not guarantee changes in the way we teach and learn. Technology should serve to enrich the educational environment, enabling the construction of knowledge through active, critical and creative action by students and teachers.

2. The hearing impaired at school

The Brazilian Federal Constitution (CFRB/88), in its article 205, ensures that education is a right for everyone, including people with disabilities, whether in a regular school environment or in specialized groups. In addition to the CFRB/88, there is other legislation in force that guarantees people with disabilities the right to education (BRASIL, 1990; BRASIL, 1993; BRASIL, 1996; BRASIL, 1997; BRASIL, 1999; BRASIL, 2001; BRASIL, 2004).

In view of the law, there is the integration of deaf people into the work and academic environment. Although the number of deaf people entering higher education institutions and companies is growing and becoming more significant every day, few institutions have adapted so that these people feel included and can participate to the point of ensuring their academic development and, consequently, their professional future. The work and academic environment is challenging for deaf people, as they still suffer from prejudice and difficulties in interacting due to the communication barrier, as there is a lack of knowledge of LIBRAS on the part of teachers and/or work colleagues.

3. Technology for special education

The use of technological aids can facilitate teaching by providing different real-world contexts in the classroom that engage and encourage students to solve complex problems (Y. Inoue, 2006).

According to the Office of Technology Assessment, most schools have one or more computers that can be used for teaching students (Mistler-Jackson, 2000).

Including technology in LS teaching and learning is the first step in encouraging children to learn something new. The next step would be to find an application that interacts with students and encourages them to study in an interactive and fun way. To do this, this project will use Augmented Reality (AR).

AR is a variation of Virtual Environments, or Virtual Reality (VR), as it is known. VR technology shows only one reality: the virtual one. When using AR, it appears that the virtual and real objects are in the same space, interacting with each other (AZUMA, 1997).

AR technologies have many applications, ranging from medical software to simulations, maintenance and so on. In this case, for education, we are using interaction with students, teachers and study material.

According to (A. Cardoso, 2007) the use of AR in the classroom is coming as a new way to minimize learning difficulties, the main problem when studying. AR technology can be used to manipulate the virtual environment, bringing information into the real world, showing 3D objects, which would be difficult to do on the blackboard or in the classroom.

In view of all the discussion, this project suggests not only learning for children with hearing difficulties or deafness. It will also serve all those who want to learn

LIBRAS in an easy and interactive way, without the need for previous training or advanced knowledge of the language.

computing. The portal with the use of AR will also be able to expand the methodologies of teachers in order to improve and innovate the teaching methods of students in a comprehensive and innovative way.

The aim of this article is to build an online portal that would be used as a dictionary, using AR technology as a way to create interest for children to learn new words in LIBRAS. To do this, 3D Avatars will be created which will behave like teachers showing how to express each word in LIBRAS. They can first be viewed as normal .gif or AR visualizations and the user can study and learn the best way to understand how the word can be expressed.

Thus, developing a portal that uses AR in the context of teaching and learning LIBRAS is an innovative project. The use of this technology is intended to provide greater interaction with the user. The aim is to make an interactive dictionary available free of charge so that anyone can learn new signs in LIBRAS in a dynamic way, with a physical-virtual interaction between the students/teachers and the study material. All you need to use this portal is a properly installed webcam, internet access and a printed marker.

4. Related work

Teaching LS connections to children in an interactive and efficient way is one of the main concerns of teachers around the world. This teaching process must be effective in allowing children to communicate with others and also to develop their own skills.

According to (Mitchell, 2011), Singel and Steven state that it is impossible to imagine life without language; it is what contributes to the main human experience, communication. Thanks to computers, many aspects of life have been modified both in field simulations and in classrooms, creating more and more interactive virtual worlds (Krummel, 1998), for new forms of teaching and learning.

There are many works that use LS, or more specifically, LIBRAS, as their teaching or comprehension principle. The work proposed in (J. E. R. Tavares, 2009) brings the SensorLIBRAS, which has an instant translation of LIBRAS signs into letters, using a glove, which sends the information of hand movements to the computer.

Recently, entrepreneur Ronaldo Tenorio created Hand Talk, an application that instantly translates a text into LS. This program has grown rapidly because it has a vast library of words, with simultaneous translation, which can be incorporated into websites to translate texts automatically.

Another way of helping deaf people is Microsoft's Kinect technology, using software developed in China. It consists of a language translator that captures hand movements with the Kinect and translates them into verbal communication. The same application is able to do the opposite, transforming the spoken language into LS with the use of an Avatar (Chen, 2013).

A game to teach LIBRAS is another way to increase interest among children. In (Magno, Machado, & Souza, 2015) the actors created an online environment, with many games, which associate .gif, the expression in LIBRAS, with a representative image. This system encourages the player to learn new words and expressions in order to complete the game.

To increase children's curiosity, researchers have proposed ELRA (LIBRAS Teaching using Augmented Reality - LIBRAS Teaching using AR). Its aim is to facilitate interaction between users without or with some degree of deafness. This program proposes the use of markers, which the children show the webcam and a virtual letter appears on the computer screen, along with its representation in LIBRAS (D. R. Nazareth, 2014).

Using AR to create educational entertainment, (L. Machado, 2013) used different types of markers that could be associated, creating a new marker symbol. From this, he created a memory game, which associates images of objects with their respective expression in LS. If the pairing was correct or incorrect, the game would display a message to the player.

5. Methodology

The project consists of creating an educational portal with great potential for learning LIBRAS for deaf students or those interested in learning the language.

In order to carry out the project, it became necessary to study how augmented reality works and to adapt this technology for the interaction and learning of deaf children in the process of acquiring LIBRAS.

AR emerges in this scenario as a new form of user interaction with the computer, creating an experience of studying with animations, which makes learning more visual, real and dynamic. This technology can be defined as a mechanism for simultaneously obtaining images, overlapping and tracking objects in virtual environments with physical environments (SISCOUTO; COSTA, 2008). It also allows users to interact with animations created by the computer through a real object.

It was also necessary to learn the signs of LIBRAS in order to interpret them in 3D animations. The regional signs of Salvador-Bahia were considered, through the DVD "Comunicando em LIBRAS" by the deaf teacher Marcos Moraes, in order to create characters that could represent the same signs, for educational purposes.

After learning LS and considering the structure in the expression of each word in LIBRAS, it became necessary to find animation and three-dimensional modeling software that could be incorporated into AR.

Finally, I wanted to research software to develop a portal that would support the implementation of these AR animations. It will serve as a dictionary for learning SL, with a search system targeted at specific themes or words.

6. Results

The *Flash Augmented Reality Authoring System (FLARAS)* tool was used to create the portal's AR environment. This tool allows 3D objects to be converted to AR, either locally or directly in the browser, using *Flash,* a webcam and a fiducial marker, as shown in figure 1.

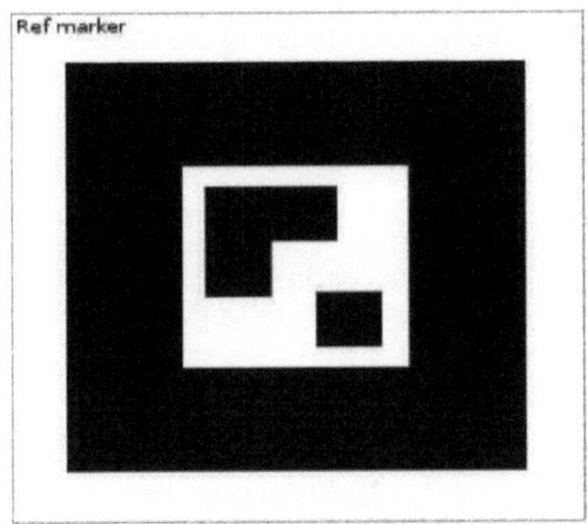

Figure 1-Marker
Source: http://ckirner.com/flaras2/download/

In the simplest applications of AR, which will be applied in this project, the computer recognizes a single real dynamic marker via a camera, allowing the creation of virtual animation. For this reason, it will not be necessary to use other markers. However, there are other, more complex ways of using this technology in the interactive scenario, giving a range of possibilities for developers and their purposes.

It was concluded that for the proposed problem, the method of a single marker allows for greater benefit from the study. This allows the user to focus on one word or expression at a time instead of watching several animations at once and not paying enough attention to each signal.

Given the complexity of the different types of sign representation, the second step was to create Avatars that would interact with the public. The idea was to find a way for those who enjoyed this new tool to identify with the Avatars and want to learn more from them. At this stage, characters of different genders and ages were modeled to represent the teachers of the portal's users.

To do this, *Makehuman* was used, *a* program that offers a pre-molded modeling interface for creating humans of all ages, as well as a vast export library.

Different puppets were then created to represent the animations in augmented reality. The interface for creating and rendering the models is shown in figures 3 and 4.

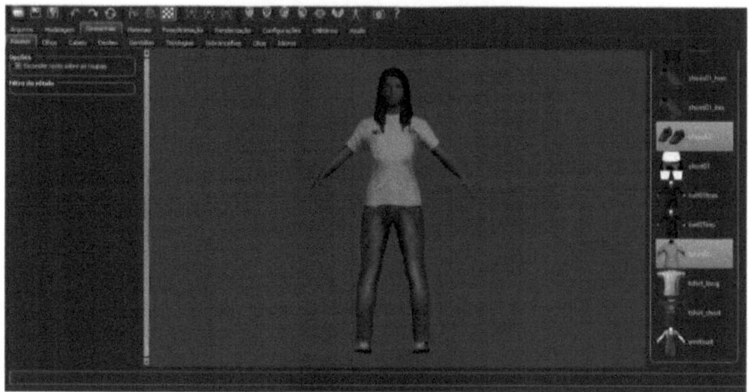

Figure 2 - Avatar modeling in Makehuman. Source: From the author (2016)

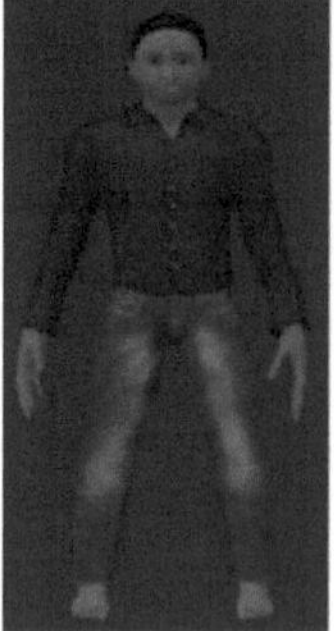

Figure 3 - Example of a rendered 3D object.
Source: from the author (2015)

The third step of the project was to animate these Avatars so that they represented the signs in LIBRAS. To do this, we used the software known as

Blender, a free tool that has a vast interface of tools for 3D manipulation and the creation of animations, as well as the option of exporting its objects to the ".dae" format, an extension understood by *FLARAS and* commonly used for three-dimensional files.

We then imported the characters modeled in *Makehuman* and, from there, we were able to implement movements in the 3D models using Blender, as shown in figure 4.

Figure 4 - Animation of the Avatars using Blender.

Source: from the author (2015)

After modeling and animating the characters, the marker was exported and associated with the animations using *FLARAS*, as can be seen in the example in figure 5.

Figure 5 - Example of a 3D object rendered on a marker using FLARAS.
Source: from the author (2015)

The Avatars loaded into *FLARAS* were adjusted in a standard way so that users could easily visualize and modify the position of each character. In addition, the program offers the user various types of adjustments, shown in figure 6, which provide different ways of adapting the Avatar to the real environment.

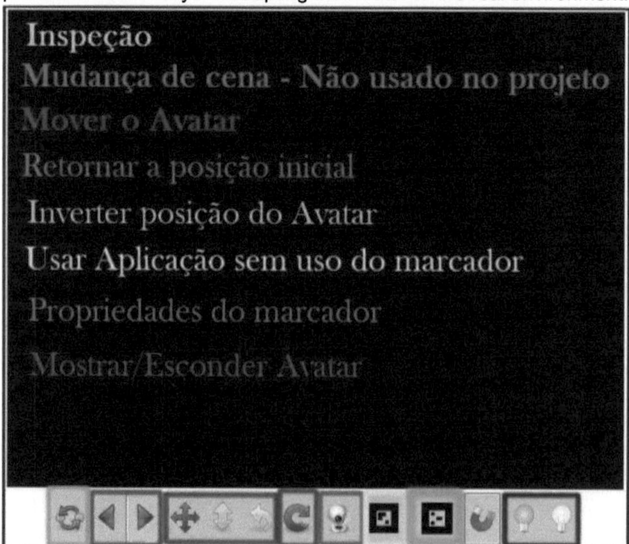

Figure 6 - Instructions for using the application.

With 3D Avatars and the use of the marker, the *FLARAS* platform provides the possibility of exporting the animation to AR with local application or directly in the *web* browser.

To use the software, when accessing the AR *interface*, the computer will ask for

permission to use the webcam (figure 7). Once permission has been granted, the AR animations are displayed.

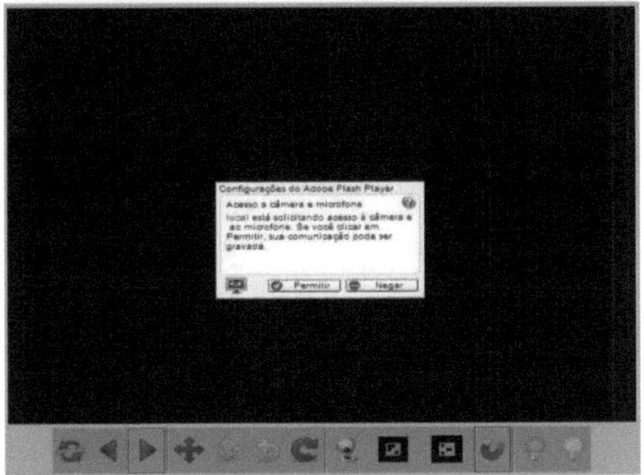

Figure 7 - Webcam permission.
Source: From the author (2015)

Below you can see some examples of Avatars created in *Makehuman* with animations made in *Blender* and exported to AR.

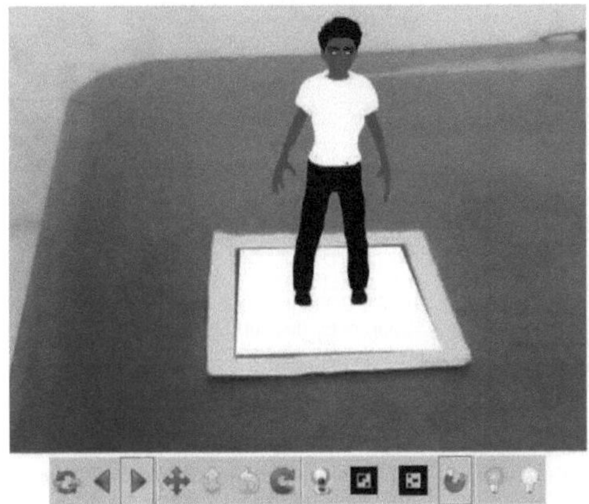

Figure 8 - Online or local Flash application with webcam permission.
Source: From the authors.

Figure 9 - ABACAXI sign[2] in
augmented reality

Source: from the author (2015)

Figure 10 - COCO sign[2] in augmented reality.
Source: by the author (2015)

---

[2] In the area of linguistic studies on LIBRAS, as a convention, researchers use a transcription system based on a form of *gloss,* i.e. words that roughly translate the meaning of the other. In our case, words from the Portuguese language were used to roughly represent statements in LIBRAS. Therefore, only some of the conventions presented by Felipe (2001) were used

Figure 11 - Watermelon sign in augmented reality.
Source: from the author (2015)

When importing the Avatars, some textures were not loaded correctly, which resulted in unexpected colors and loss of sharpness of expression, as can be seen in figure 12.

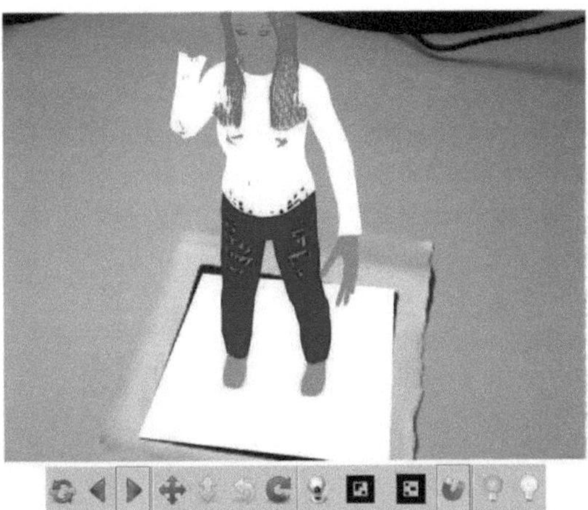

Figure 12 - Avatar texture flaw. Source: by the author (2015)

To mitigate the flaw, we tried to remove the textures and details from the characters, as well as using the primary colors, black and white, as can be seen in figure 13.

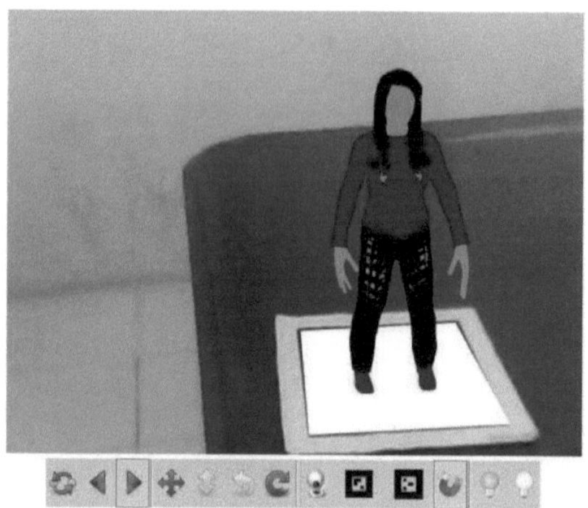

Figure 13- Use of primary colors.
Source: from the author (2015)

There was an improvement in the image, but it was still not possible to see the Avatars' facial expressions clearly. This can be a problem for some signs, as a large part of the message conveyed using LS is conveyed with facial expressions.

After a few more tests with children and some teachers dedicated to LIBRAS education, we also saw the possibility of bringing the animations closer together to make the Avatar's face and hands more visible, since in LS the legs are not used. This change was applied and can be seen in figure 14.

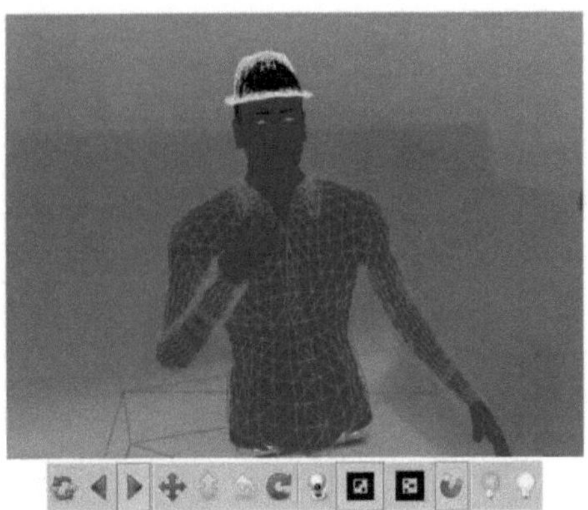

Figure 14 - Thunderstorm sign in augmented reality.
Source: from the author (2015)

Despite the improvement in understanding the signs using gestures, the facial expressions were still not clear. Taking this as the basis of the problem, we looked for a way to modify the methodology of this work.

After several attempts, all of which were unsuccessful, we tried to change the basis of the Avatar modeling. To do this, we used ready-made Avatars from the *3D Warehouse* - a Google library that makes available various 3D objects free of charge created by various 3D modeling developers around the world.

Figure 15 - Avatar ready for 3D Warehouse Google
Source: From the author (2016)

Despite the good results in the Avatar textures from the *Warehouse* 3D library, difficulties were encountered in modeling and animating the characters. This was due to the fact that this library uses fixed textures and poses which made it difficult to implement skeletons, the basis of movement in *Blender*, and thus to create movement, especially when trying to put expressions on the characters.

Because of this, we looked for another platform capable of creating, modeling and animating the models that was compatible with *Blender* and *Flaras.* The third option chosen was *DAZ Studio* (a program capable of creating characters with high quality and performance). The program is free, but in order to get the most out of it, with more creation and development options, it is necessary to pay.

Due to its ready-made interface, high compatibility with *Blender* and, finally, good recognition of Avatars in AR, the free version of the program was chosen. We then created 2 different characters, as shown in figures 16 and 17.

Figure 16 - Male avatar created in DAZ Studio. Source: From the author (2016).

Figure 17 - Female avatar created in DAZ Studio. Source: by the author (2016).

Once imported into *Blender*, these models began to be animated. However, as a way of improving the expression of the characters, we started using the tool known as Motion Capture (MOCAP) which is also offered within the *Blender* interface. This tool allows characters to follow the movements of markers in videos or footage. This gives the Avatar a more natural and human way of moving.

Image 18 shows an example of a MOCAP implementation. The quality of the recorded video has been reduced and its colors have been set to black and white to make it easier to recognize the markers that have been placed on the face. As MOCAP recognition was done using simple videos (taken with a 20.7 megapixel SONY Xperia Z2 cell phone camera) and *Blender* doesn't have a very good

and Blender doesn't have a good entertainment of MOCAP with 3D movements, it was decided to use this tool only to detect the expressions of the face and not the entire movement of the body.

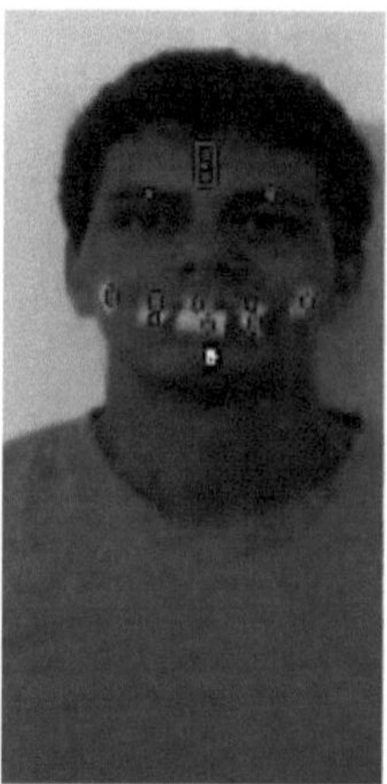

Figure 18 - Face recognition using Blender's MOCAP.
Source: From the author (2016)

The tapes contained in the rest serve to facilitate computer recognition of the points that are being moved and which must be passed on to the virtual character. The recorded movements are then passed on to the Avatar.

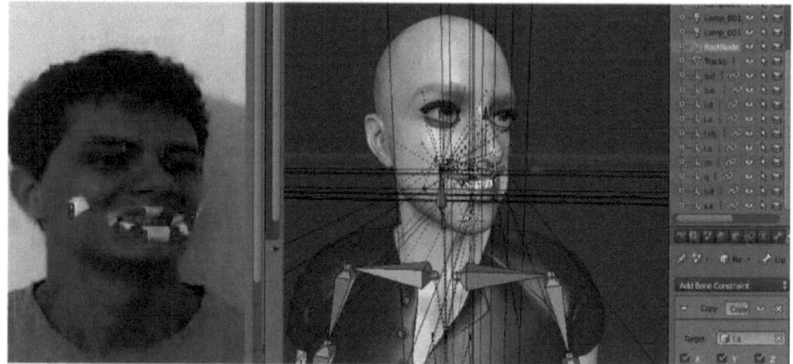

Figure 19 - Recognition of movements by the Avatar through Blender's MOCAP. Source: From the author (2016)

Once these new animations were created, they were uploaded *to FLARAS*, transforming them into AR.

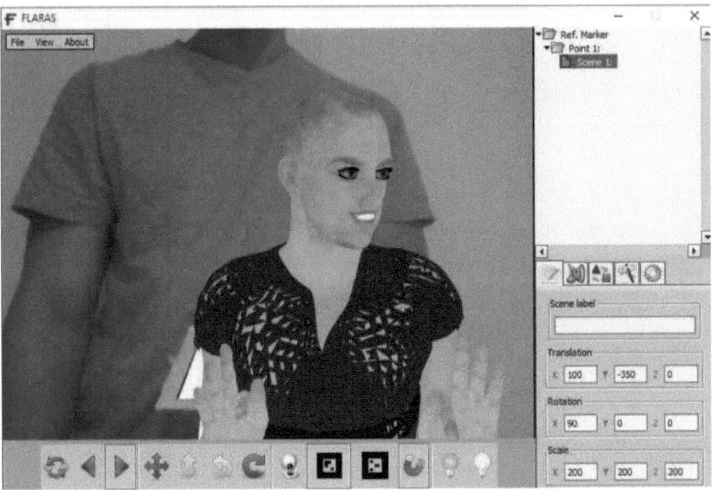

Figure 20 - AR animation of the Avatar uploaded to Flaras (Happy in LIBRAS).
Source: From the author (2016)

Images 21 and 22 show how the movements of Avatar in AR match up with the movement of the filmed markers.

Figure 21 - Comparison of the object in Augmented Reality with the expression made in MOCAP. Signal referring to heat.
Source: From the author (2016)

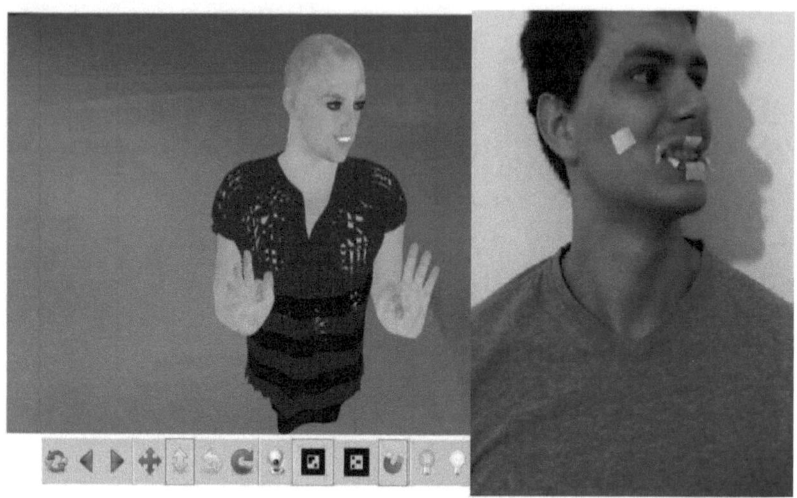

Figure 22 - Comparison of the object in Augmented Reality with the expression made in MOCAP. Sign referring to happiness.
Source: From the author (2016)

It is important to emphasize that the lighting, fullness of the marker, focus and quality of the webcam is related to the speed and recognition of the marker as a reference object for AR. To improve this recognition, it is recommended that the study site is properly lit and that the marker is printed on a sheet of cardboard or glued to a piece of cardboard. Based on this, figure 23 shows a suggestion for creating a studio in which the study can be carried out with fewer obstacles.

Figure 23 - Studio for a better focus on animation.
Source: from the author (2015)

The last part of this project consisted of creating an academic portal that supported all the augmented reality animations and had a simple, interactive interface. To do this, we used the *Wordpress* tool, a platform focused on creating websites or blogs with high performance and aesthetics.

The portal developed shows an environment full of themes to choose from, in which the person using it can search for specific content or animations and learn or check the gesture movement for that sign. With the chosen word, you can see the LIBRAS sign in animation in a 2D environment, where you can focus more on the correct position of the hand in relation to the body and the expressions of the animated characters. By clicking on the 3D environment, the user, using a marker and camera, will see the animation previously seen, in a 3D environment that interacts with the position of the marker. From a fixed position of the student's choice, they can remove the marker, or not, and pay attention to the dynamics of the animation to better study each word.

On the portal's home page (figure 24) you can download and print the bookmark that will be used to visualize the figures in AR.

Figure 24 - Portal home page.
Source: From the author (2015)

In the augmented reality animations section (figure 25) there is a menu with various themes already created.

Figure 25 - Page layout and menus.
Source: From the author (2015)

By choosing a word, the user is directed to a page where the meaning of the word is stated with a brief demonstration of the AR animation being displayed as a 2D animation (figure 26).

The portal also has a page where all the latest news uploaded to each theme and the new themes created are displayed (figure 27 and 28).

Figure 26 - Page showing an animated .gif with a link to augmented reality.
Source: From the author (2015)

Figure 27 - Updating the portal's feelings theme.
Source: From the author (2016)

Figure 28 - New page referring to sentiment themes on the Portal. Source: From the author (2016)

The portal can be accessed in the classroom, at home, or any other environment where there is *internet,* a webcam and the bookmark that is available on the portal for *download.* The portal's interface is very simple and seeks to select animations via themes and search systems.

To load all the AR animations on the web pages with the standard formatting, we used the internal *FLARAS* code, as shown in figure 29.

```xml
<?xml version="1.0" encoding="utf-8" ?>
- <objectsList>
  - <object3D>
      <idNumber>1</idNumber>
      <label />
      <filePath>dae/coco/obj3dFile.dae</filePath>
    - <translation>
        <x>0</x>
        <y>0</y>
        <z>0</z>
      </translation>
    - <rotation>
        <x>90</x>
        <y>0</y>
        <z>0</z>
      </rotation>
    - <scale>
        <x>30</x>
        <y>30</y>
        <z>30</z>
      </scale>
    - <texture>
        <hasTexture>0</hasTexture>
        <texturePath />
        <width>0</width>
        <height>0</height>
      </texture>
    - <audio>
        <hasAudio>0</hasAudio>
        <audioPath />
        <repeatAudio>0</repeatAudio>
      </audio>
    - <video>
        <hasVideo>0</hasVideo>
        <videoPath />
        <width>0</width>
        <height>0</height>
        <repeatVideo>0</repeatVideo>
      </video>
    - <animation>
        <hasAnimation>0</hasAnimation>
        <type>0</type>
      </animation>
```

Figure 29 - Incorporating AR objects into the academic portal.
Source: From the author (2015)

Finally, some of the animations added to the portal can be seen in figures 30, 31 and 32.

Figure 30 - Feeling: Sad. Source: From the author (2016)

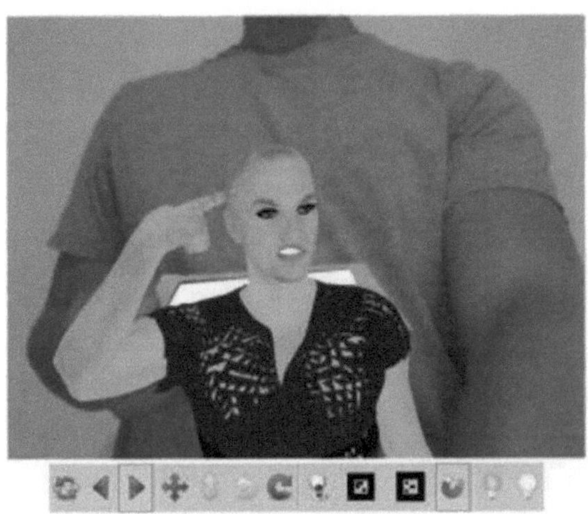

Figure 31 - Feeling: Headache in AR.
Source: From the author (2016)

Figure 32 - Feeling: Heat in AR.
Source: From the author (2016)

The difficulty of loading textures continued, however, thanks to the use of *DAZ Studio* a better result was achieved. Below you can compare two animations, one using the textures provided by *Makehuman* and the other provided by *DAZ Studio,* when implemented in AR.

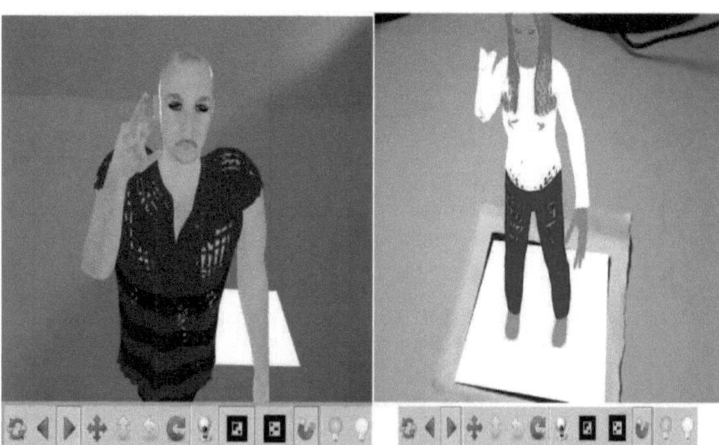
Figure 33 - Comparison between the avatars made in DAZ Studio and Makehuman.
Source: From the author (2016)

Avatars can be placed in any position, allowing users to create their own learning dynamics and interact in the way they find most convenient.

Figure 34 - Demonstration of how to interact with the
Avatar.
Source: From the author (2017)

Figure 35 - Demonstration of how to interact with the
Avatar.
Source: From the author (2017)

According to the results, there was a significant improvement in understanding the signs. The use of MOCAP enabled the recognition of human facial expressions which were successfully implemented in the Avatars.

After the work was completed, some tests were carried out with people who use the language and with children without AD who have LIBRAS classes at school. They quickly adapted to and were curious about the movements of the virtual characters. After testing some of the words shown on the portal, it was observed that the children stopped several times a day to perform the movements they didn't know, as well as showing their classmates, who hadn't seen the animations, the meaning of the words they had learned in LIBRAS.

Figure 36 - Interaction of a child without AD with the portal. Source: From the author (2016)

Figure 37 - Interaction with the portal by a child without AD.
Source: From the author (2016)

For future work, it is still important to focus on improving the sharpness of the characters, as well as implementing the use of MOCAP to a greater extent, which, in this project, proved to be very effective in producing more realistic animations. Perhaps with the use of better equipment it will be possible for animations to be made instantly using only MOCAP and then to implement these animations in AR using *Flaras*. Another important aspect of this project is the need to keep children's attention on the portal for longer. As a result, the aim of future projects is to create games that use the portal's AR library to further entertain those interested in learning LIBRAS.

7. Final considerations

The portal developed seeks to create a new form of teaching and interaction for learning LIBRAS. This project sought to create animations focused on LIBRAS, taking into account the signs used in the city of Salvador-Bahia, in various specific daily themes, using AR technology for study.

It is hoped that the user will learn new LIBRAS signs and be able to watch the animations as many times as necessary. What's more, all you need to use the portal *is internet* access, a simple webcam and the use of a marker, making it an easy-to-use tool that can be viewed in schools, homes, universities and other environments. These animations were tested with the LIBRAS teacher at IFBA who approved the understanding of the signs. As well as being very useful for the IFBA community, it will be a portal available to various students interested in learning LS, whether they are users of the gestures or interested in learning to communicate with people who use sign language.

The inclusion of MOCAP in this work was able to bring more expression to the Avatars. This has transformed the characters into more human beings, who show, through the expression of their faces, feelings and anguish by gesturing words such as pain and happiness, for example. This factor is very important in LS, as it is the expressions that give meaning and intonation to the speech being passed on.

The application study of the portal proved to be very productive in terms of its use by educators, children and teenagers who did or did not have any kind of orientation on LIBRAS. The distraction imposed on the children when using the platform created an attraction for knowledge, which encouraged them to learn more words and spread this form of learning to their peers.

In the future developments of this project we intend to improve some aspects of the portal as well as extending the number of animations and themes for it. Improving the visualization and animation of the 3D Avatars in augmented reality is still a challenge to be overcome. Perhaps, with the use of better technical resources, it will be possible to improve the expressions displayed, making the creation of new animations more dynamic and agile. With these improvements, users of the portal will be able to access a vast number of new words with good quality for learning.

Bibliographical references

A. CARDOSO; C. K. (2007). **Technologies for the development of virtual and augmented reality systems**. Recife: Ed. Universitaria da UFPE.

AZUMA, R. T. (1997). **A survey of augmented reality**. Presence: Teleoperators and Virtual Environments, 355-385.

BARROS, A. C. T.; GALINDO, M. A. C.; JACOB, R. T. S. **Knowledge and conduct of pediatricians regarding hearing impairment**. Pediatrics, v. 24, n. 1/2, p. 25-31, 2002. Available at:
<http://pediatriasaopaulo.usp.br/upload/pdf/550.pdf> Accessed on: 10/12/14.

BENTO, N. A. **Phonological parameters: hand configuration, articulation point and movement in the acquisition of Brazilian sign language - a case study**. 2010, 143f. 74f. Dissertation (Master's Degree) - Institute of Letters, Federal University of Bahia - UFBA, Salvador, 2010.

BRASIL. **Constituigao**: Constitution of the Federative Republic of Brazil: constitutional text promulgated on October 5, 1988, as amended by Constitutional Amendments Nos. 1/92 to 46/2005 and by Constitutional Amendments No. 1 to 6/94. Brasilia: Senado Federal; Subsecretaria de Edigoes Tecnicas, 2005.

BRAZIL. Decree No. 2.208, of April 17, 1997. Regulates §2 of art. 36 and arts. 39 to 42 of Law no. 9.394, of December 20, 1996, which establishes the guidelines and bases of national education. **Official Gazette of the Federative Republic of Brazil.** Brasilia, DF, 18 abr. 1997. Available at:
<http://www.planalto.gov.br/ccivil_03/decreto/D2208.htm> Accessed on: 19/04/15.

BRAZIL. Decree No. 3.298, of December 20, 1999. Regulates Law No. 7.853, of October 24, 1989, provides for the National Policy for the Integration of Persons with Disabilities, consolidates protection rules, and makes other provisions. **Official Gazette of the Federative Republic of Brazil.** Brasilia, DF, Dec. 21, 1999. Available at: <
http://www.planalto.gov.br/ccivil_03/decreto/D3298.htm> Accessed on: 19/04/15.

BRAZIL. Decree No. 914, of September 6, 1993. Institutes the National Policy for the Integration of People with Disabilities, and other measures. **Official Gazette of the Federative Republic of Brazil.** Brasilia, DF,
8 Sept. 1993. Available at: <
http://www.planalto.gov.br/ccivil_03/decreto/D0914.htm> Accessed on: 19/04/15.

BRAZIL. Law No. 10.172, of January 9, 2001. Approves the National Education Plan and other measures. **Official Gazette of the Federative Republic of Brazil.** Brasilia, DF, January 10, 2001. Available at: <
https://www.planalto.gov.br/ccivil_03/leis/leis_2001/l10172.htm> Accessed on: 19/04/15.

BRAZIL. Law No. 10.845, of March 5, 2004. Establishes the Program to

Complement Specialized Educational Assistance for People with Disabilities, and makes other provisions. **Official Gazette of the Federative Republic of Brazil.** Brasilia, DF, March 8, 2004. Available at: < ftp://ftp.fnde.gov.br/web/resolucoes_2004/lei10845_05032004.pdf> Accessed on: 19/04/15.

BRAZIL. Law No. 8.069, of July 13, 1990. Provides for the Statute of the Child and Adolescent and other measures. **Official Gazette of the Federative Republic of Brazil.** Brasilia, DF, July 16, 1990. Available at: < http://www.planalto.gov.br/ccivil_03/LEIS/L8069.htm > Accessed on: 19/04/15.

BRAZIL. Law No. 9.394, of December 20, 1996. Establishes the guidelines and bases of national education. **Official Gazette of the Federative Republic of Brazil.** Brasilia, DF, December 23, 1996. Available at: < http://www.planalto.gov.br/ccivil_03/Leis/L9394.htm > Accessed on: 19/04/15.

CASTRO JUNIOR, G. **Linguistic variation in Brazilian Sign Language: focus on the lexicon.** UnB, 2011. Available at: < http://repositorio.unb.br/bitstream/10482/8859/1/2011_GI%C3%A1uciodeCastro J%C3%BAnior.pdf> Accessed on: 10/12/14.

Chen, X. H. (2013). **Kinect Sign Language Translator expands communication possibilities.** Microsoft Research Connections.

D. R. Nazareth, M. A. (2014). **ELRA - Teaching Libras using Augmented Reality.** XVI Symposium on Virtual and Augmented Reality.

DE BRITO, A. M|. W.; DESSEN, M. A. **Deaf children and their families: an overview.** Federal University of Rio Grande do Sul, 1999. Available at: < http://www.scielo.br/scielo.php?script=sci_arttext&pid=S0102-79721999000200012> Accessed on: 10/12/14.From Sao Paulo. Creator of Hand Talk is among the most promising young people in Brazil; Available at:<

http://www1 .folha.uol.com.br/empreendedorsocial/2016/03/1746569-criador-do-hand-talk-esta- entre-os-jovens-mais-promissores-do-brasil.shtml> Accessed: 01/06/2017

FELIPE, T. A; MONTEIRO, M. S. **Libras em Contexto: curso basico, livro do professor instrutor** - Brasilia: Programa Nacional de Apoio a Educagao dos Surdos, MEC: SEESP, 2001.

J. E. R. Tavares, V. L. (2009). **An application for teaching Portuguese to the deaf using the Libras sensor.** Anais do Simposio Brasileiro de Informatica na Educagao.

KIRNER, C. **Virtual and augmented reality**; Available at: <http://www.ckirner.com/realidadevirtual/>Accessed on: 10/12/14.

Krummel, T. M. (1998). **Surgical simulation and virtual reality: the coming revolution.** Annals of surgery, 635.

L. Machado, M. M. (2013). **Development of a memory game using augmented reality for the teaching-learning process of the deaf and hard** of hearing. **CONAHPA**. Joao Pessoa: Hypermedia and Interdisciplinarity in the generation of knowledge.

Livadas, G. (2013). **Deaf Education**: A New Philosophy. Rocheste, New York, USA.

Magno, R. S., Machado, L. C., & Souza, A. C. (2015). **Development of an interactive portal of animations for the teaching-learning process of the Brazilian Sign Language (LIBRAS)**. CONAHPA. Sao Luis: Hypermedia and Interdisciplinarity in the generation of knowledge.

MAINART, D. A.; SANTOS, C. M. **The importance of technology in the teaching-learning process**. Faculdade Presidente Antonio Carlos and UFVJM ; Available at:
<http://www.convibra.com.br/upload/paper/adm/adm_1201 .pdf> Accessed on 14/01/14

MARISE, I. **What do you know about augmented reality**. 2013. Available at: <http://vamosestudarcsj.blogspot.com.br/2013/02/voce-sabe-o-que-e-augmented-reality.html> Accessed on: 10/12/14.

Mistler-Jackson, M. a. (2000). **Student motivation and Internet technology: Are students empowered to learn science?** Journal of Research in Science Teaching, 459-479.

Mitchell, K. (2011). **Perspectives: The Language Deaf...What's Really Wrong with Deaf Education**. The Endeavor, 47-48.

MORAN, J. M. **New technologies and the re-enchantment of the world**. Educational Technology Magazine. Rio de Janeiro, vol. 23, n2. p.126, Sep/Oct 1995

PEIXOTO, R. C. **Algumas considerapoes sobre a interface entre a lingua brasileira de sinais (LIBRAS) e a lingua portuguesa na construção inicial da escrita pela criança surda**. Cad. Cedes, v. 26, n. 69, p. 205-229, 2006. Available at: <http://www.scielo.br/scielo.php?script=sci_arttext&pid=S0101-32622006000200006> Accessed on: 10/12/14.

RAMOS, C. R. AZUL, Executive Director of Editora Arara. **LIBRAS: the sign language of deaf Brazilians**. Petropolis-RJ, Editora Arara Azul, 2006. Available at: < http://www.editora-arara-azul.com.br/pdf/artigo2.pdf> Accessed on: 10/12/14.

REDONDO, M. C. F.; CARVALHO, J. M. **Deficiencia Auditiva**. In: Cadernos da TV Escola. N° 1,2000.

FENEIS MAGAZINE. Numbers 1 to 13. R.J. 1999/2002.

SISCOUTO, R; COSTA, R. (Org.). **Virtual and augmented reality: a technological approach**. Porto Alegre: Brazilian Computer Society, SBC, 2008.

SOUZA, R.C.; MOREIRA, H.D.F.; KIRNER, C. **- FLARAS 1.0 - Flash Augmented Reality Authoring System, e-book, 2012**. Available at:

<http://ckirner.com/flaras2/wp-content/uploads/2012/09/livro-flaras.pdf>. Accessed on: 10/12/14.

SOUZA, R.C.; MOREIRA, H.D.F.; KIRNER, C. **FLARAS 2.4.3**; Available at: <http://ckirner.com/flaras2/> Accessed on: 10/12/14.

World Health Organization (May 30, 2017). **Deafness and hearing loss.** Available at: < http://www.who.int/mediacentre/factsheets/fs300/en/> Accessed on: 10/12/14.

Y. Inoue, S. T. **Teaching with Educational Technology in the 21st Century**: The case of the Asia-Pacific Region. Idea Group, 30.2006

SZILLAT, R. R.; DINIZ, M. V. C. D; MACHADO, L. C. **Development of an augmented reality animation portal for the teaching-learning process of the Brazilian Sign Language - LIBRAs.** CONAHPA 2015. Sao Luis: Hypermedia and Interdisciplinarity in the Generation of Knowledge.

SZILLAT, R. R.; DINIZ, M. V. C. D; MACHADO, L. C. **Using the FLATOORKIT framework to create learning methods and objects for deaf students who use sign language.** XII SICTI 2015

SZILLAT, R. R.; MACHADO, L. C. **Using the FLATOORKIT framework to create methods and learning objects for deaf students who use sign language.** XIII SICTI 2016

Summary

yes **I want** morebooks!

Buy your books fast and straightforward online - at one of world's fastest growing online book stores! Environmentally sound due to Print-on-Demand technologies.

Buy your books online at
www.morebooks.shop

Kaufen Sie Ihre Bücher schnell und unkompliziert online – auf einer der am schnellsten wachsenden Buchhandelsplattformen weltweit! Dank Print-On-Demand umwelt- und ressourcenschonend produziert.

Bücher schneller online kaufen
www.morebooks.shop

info@omniscriptum.com
www.omniscriptum.com

Printed by Books on Demand GmbH, Norderstedt / Germany